CHIEDOZIE EZE

Teenagers of the Bible

Bible Lessons For The Contemporary Teen

Teenagers
of the
Bible

CHIEDOZIE EZE

Teenagers
of the
Bible

Copyright © 2021 by Chiedozie

All rights reserved.

APPRECIATIONS

I return all honour to God for the inspiration and grace that has resulted in the expressions found in this book. To him alone be all the glory.

And to the excellent team at TEEN SUCCESS ACADEMY, Grace and Joshua. Thank you for putting up with my excesses to see that this book is a reality. Many thanks to all the teenagers and parents that have trusted us to be a part of their journey. We do not take the honour lightly.

To my coach on this journey, Wendy Ologe. Thank you for taking a chance on me and for insisting that "this book must come out."

Thank you to all the coaches, mentors and friends who have been of immense support to me. To all of you who took time to read through the content and share your inputs and reviews. I do not take it for granted.

Thanks to Irene, and the amazing team at Oasis for helping to get this out work on schedule.

DEDICATION

This book is dedicated to every young person who is daring to be different, living a life of impact to transform society.

FOREWORD

It is true that the work of raising children is very tasking. The Bible acknowledges this difficult reality in Proverbs 22:15: "Folly is bound up in the heart of a child". The Bible also offers parents the promise that wisdom can eventually replace folly in a child's heart. "Train up a child in a way he should go, so when he is old, he will not depart from it" (Proverbs 22:6).

As parents, one of the most important skills you can teach your teen is the renewing of his/her mind. The mistake many parents make is to try to renew their teen's mind for them. Renewing the mind is a day-to-day process of thinking biblically. This can be made easy and interesting to the children by using certain teenagers of the Bible for quick illustration to look at the things they did and how these things impacted their lives either positively or negatively and the lessons to learn.

In this book, the author has made a selection of such teenagers to make this work more practical, at the same time an interesting thing to do. These teenagers include: Abel and Cain, Esau and Jacob, Joseph, David, Josiah, Esther, Daniel and the three Hebrew boys – Shadrach, Meshach and Abednego, Mary the mother of Jesus and even Jesus Christ himself. These were teenagers whose characters at one point or the other were used to teach others, either to emulate or desist from.

Going by this therefore, there is a great lesson to be learnt by studying the lives of these Bible figures in their teenage ages and using their experiences and lessons as a guide in our own lives as teenagers.

The author has done a noble job in putting up this masterpiece which happened to be a huge gap that needed to be filled in the lives of our teens, particularly in the times we are currently in. He has pinpointed the most appealing Bible teenagers to drive this message even deeper, and to give a much understandable meaning. This is one material every parent, teenager, teacher and caregiver must have. The message contained herein is worth teaching to every teenager whose value is that of living the life that is pleasing to God.

Wendy Ologe

Author/Parent Coach

Founder of The Intentional Parent Academy

PRAISE FOR *TEENAGERS OF THE BIBLE*

In every generation, God had always used people in their teenage years to start a series of events that would affect the course of history and eternity. Whether these people be a Joseph, Daniel, or the maid that told king Naaman about the healing power of God.

'Teenagers of the Bible' would attempt to give us a sneak peek into the lives of those God used in time past, and also those that missed it in life because they missed it as teenagers.

Above all, the book would bring us timely and applicable insights into "weaponizing" the teenagers that God will use as agents of transformation and social change in every sector of society and every nation of the world. Welcome to an adventure into a life of positive generational influence.

_Obed Kure
Lead Pastor, Ignite Christian Centre, Jos.

TEENAGERS OF THE BIBLE - A book whose title may appear simple but whose content is powerful.

I receive a lot of calls from parents asking for my help with their teenagers. "Why is he behaving this way?" they would often ask. I wish that this book was written earlier, as it provides the answers these parents seek.

Presented in a storytelling format, the book captivates, not just by providing crucial answers, but guidance for the youth and teenagers of today, as well as their parents. As future leaders, it is a collective effort to ensure every young man and woman receives the proper knowledge and nurture. A must-read for parents and teenagers!

_Mr. Kingsley Madu
CEO, Expedier Group
Teens Advocate/Trainer, Canada.

*TEENAGERS OF THE BIBLE —lessons for the contemporary teen by Chiedozie...*is a timely masterpiece that comes in a period where the millennial teen is in dire need of role models that exemplify Godly virtues void of the present moral decay that has bedeviled our contemporary world. This book should be in the hand of every teenager that desires and dares to be different, unique & whole.

_Ernest Azu
Chief Executive Officer, HYPE Foundation

Growing up as a teenager, I was in the midst of a group of young men who were deeply rooted in Christ and continuously strove to be like Him. I was in the midst of young girls who carried themselves like those who lived in the palace and desperately desired to make it a reality. Teenagers in these groups were modeling after other youths in the bible like Joseph, Esther, Daniel, etc. Bible study time was a fun time as we all desired to get rhema from God's word.

Today, teenagers say the bible is boring and have no desire to read, meditate or practice the word. Unfortunately, this has done them no good as they have made many grievous mistakes they could have avoided if they read their bibles.

'TEENAGERS OF THE BIBLE' is here to the rescue. A book to stir up the interest of our teenagers to go back to their source—God's word is what every teen needs.

Youths love stories and easy-to-read and easy-to-understand lessons, and they would love this masterpiece. Studying these bible characters, I believe, would spark their interest, and soon they will have an unquestionable fire for the bible to the glory of God.

This resource is a blessing directly from heaven to our generation at such a time as this. Hallelujah!!

_Etima Abang Umeh
Teen Mentor, Responsible Teens Academy

In an era when young people desperately need godly peers, mentors, and coaches, the book, *Teenagers of the Bible* is an answer to the heart cries of many youths and their parents. It is a collection of well-researched and richly developed stories of young people in the Bible. This uncommon, powerful, and thought-provoking page-turner extracts vital life lessons from Bible Teens, relevant to both the young and old. The review questions after each character study reiterated the message in a format that left me in a self-appraisal mode.

The book is so easy to read, simple to understand, and the stories are very relatable. *"Discretion will preserve you; Understanding will keep you, to deliver you from the way of evil..."* from the story of Joseph is so profound and relevant, especially in these times when caution is often thrown to the wind.

Chiedozie does a fantastic job highlighting important principles that would distinguish any young person in all spheres of life. If you are a parent, parent-to-be, teenager, teen-worker, or just passionate about raising a unique generation for Christ, then this book is definitely for you!

_Chiagoziem Adindu
CEO, Educate The Citizens International Organization (ETCIO)

As a youth pastor, I have been on a mad search for Godly yet creative books for teenagers. The *"TEENAGERS OF THE BIBLE"* is an inspiring book and hits the mark for quality teenage reading, but this book was also fun to read. The engaging language is teenage-centered, and I was happy to have a story from the Bible that has not been overdone. I recommend this book for every young person to read.

_Pst. Nwamuo Emmanuel
Youth/Teens Pastor, Streams of Joy. Nottingham, United Kingdom.

The bible is a compendium of wisdom. Chiedozie has extracted the best illustrations from the bible and transformed it into a self-improvement tool for young people. The practical wisdom contained in this book will help every teenager deal with daily challenges. I recommend it.

_Sam Udemezue.
Performance Auditor, Canada.

As a young person, one of the reasons I wanted to go into the law profession was one of my favorite bible characters —Deborah.

According to the Book of Judges, Deborah was a prophetess of the God of the Israelites: the fourth judge of pre-monarchic Israel, the only female judge mentioned in the Bible, and equally the wife of Lapidoth. Deborah is one of the most influential women of the Bible, excelling in multiple areas with outstanding leadership qualities. Her story influenced me growing up.

However, if we ask our teenagers in this generation who their role models are, I'm sure none of the Bible characters will come tops. What we hear are the names of musicians, actors, influencers, etcetera. And little wonder why our morals are seriously lacking. We are dealing with a deficiency in values and principles because we have left our foundations in the Bible to go after mundane things. That is why I'm super happy with this book, '*TEENAGERS OF THE BIBLE —Lessons for the contemporary teenager.*'

It is a timely book, and I wish our religious organizations would order as many thousands of copies as possible and give it to our teenagers. As the circular world is working very hard to win over our younger generation, we should go the extra mile as well.

Uncle Chiedozie, thank you so much for this timely piece. I believe you will exceed your heart's desires for this book. God bless you, Coach.

_Aunty Chichi Umeseaka
Social Worker/Teen Coach/Mentor/Therapist/OAP/TV Show Host,
and Producer.
Special Adviser to Abia State Governor.

The world is fast evolving and there is an urgent need to start paying keen attention to a world where our children's future is being uprooted at the early stage of their lives; where sons and daughters do not grow to become authentic men and virtuous women who are ready and capable to become change agents at any given sphere they find themselves.

This is a very timely and unique book that focuses on studies that attempt to x-ray the lives of both successful and dishonorable teenagers in the Bible as I recall the words of Apostle Paul when He wrote to His Mentee 'Timothy' in 2 Timothy 3:16 and I quote "All scripture is given by inspiration of God, and is profitable for doctrine, for reproof, for correction, for instruction in righteousness."

This is not just a book for parents and teenagers; rather, it is a book for parents who are eager to know principles of child upbringing that have stood the test of time based on past successes and failures. It is a book for any Teenager who desires to be an OAK or an EAGLE wherever they find themselves at any given time.

And yes, Dozie specifically wrote this book for you; the boy or girl who wants to be the strength and hope of their family and a blessing to their society by upholding the truth and integrity of God.

_Olorunisola AbdulJelil Olapade, FIMC CMC
Dominion City, Lagos

Table of Contents

SONS AND DAUGHTERS
– A Parent's Prayer

11Rid me, and deliver me from the hand of strange children, Whose mouth speaketh vanity, and their right hand *is* a right hand of falsehood:

12That our sons *may be* as plants grown up in their youth;

***That* our daughters *may be* as cornerstones, polished *after* the similitude of a palace:**

13 *That* our garners *may be* full, affording all manner of store: *That* our sheep may bring forth thousands and ten thousands in our streets:

14 *That* our oxen *may be* strong to labour;

That there be no breaking in, nor going out; That *there be* no complaining in our streets.

15Happy *is that* people, that is in such a case: *Yea*, happy *is that* people, whose God *is* the LORD.

INTRODUCTION

The blessings of God as promised in Deuteronomy chapter 28 include the "fruit of your body," which refers to your children. In the scripture above, the Psalmist prays not just for sons and daughters but for a certain quality of sons and daughters.

Sons as plants grown up in their youth:

The metaphor drawn here is a picture of an oak tree - sturdy, well-rooted, with a thick stem to support its height, branches, and full leaves. It is a picture of stability, resourcefulness, spiritual and physical health.

This kind of "tree" can withstand the elements in different climates and environments. His faculties are developed in multiple directions - emotional, intellectual, vocational, and otherwise. He can stand the blasts of life's strong winds and difficulties, and his branches are comfortable enough for the birds to make their nest. He is not a terror but a source of grace to the family and everyone that encounters him.

They are the strength and hope of every family and a blessing to society.

With the growing rate of depression and suicide in our society, we need the kind of youth that is not overwhelmed by the vicissitudes of life. A young man whose mind is girded with truth can find strength for himself and others around him. He stands tall in the city unintimidated among his peers.

Blessed is the parent who has this kind of son, "They shall not be ashamed but shall speak with their enemies in the gate."

Daughters as pillars (cornerstones) sculptured after the similitude of the palace:

Pillars and cornerstones - again, we see a picture of strength mixed with beauty and grace. Different parts of a building are connected and united by the strength of cornerstones and pillars. This daughter is strong in body, spirit, and mind.

After the similitude of the palace - the word palace is also interpreted as a temple. If you've ever seen a picture of ancient temples, they were architectural masterpieces and you'd wonder how those structures were conceived, designed, and constructed. The sheer size and skillful artworks carved on stones.

This work of art is intricately beautiful, yet so strong, the weight and very survival of the entire building depend on it. This daughter is prepared (fashioned, polished) for no ordinary house, but a palace. She is noble, polished in character, and able to lead. The strength, happiness, and emotional security of her family depend on her.

The sad history, however, is that cruel cultures and religions have destroyed the image of the girl child. A similar fate has befallen the sons too with massive loss of masculinity destroying families and society at large.

The cry to restore this image in our sons and daughters should be the focus of development for godly youth.

May God help us to raise a generation of sons and daughters that possess these qualities.

I imagine our families like beautiful palaces and our cities adorned with oaks. Charles Spurgeon said, "A city built up of such dwellings is a city of palaces, and a state composed of such cities is a republic of princes."

The following chapters are personal bible studies - an attempt to x-ray the lives of successful (and the dishonourable) teenagers of the bible. Perhaps, our generation will learn a thing or two to help us in becoming oaks and pillars.

Chiedozie Eze
November, 2021

1. CAIN AND ABEL - A STORY ABOUT SIBLING SQUABBLES

Reference: Genesis 4:1-16

Isn't it quite strange that the first homicide case in human history was recorded as early as in chapter four of the story? I think it is. Now that goes to tell you how badly the knowledge of evil can affect humans.

The fight started with an offering to God by two guys. Cain and Abel are brothers, teenagers by this time. The other thing we are told is that they both had an occupation. Abel was a shepherd, rearing sheep while Cain was a farmer.

In the course of time, Cain and Abel each brought offerings to the Lord. Offering means giving back to God, it's an act of worship, love, gratitude, and devotion.

The story says that God had respect for Abel and his offering while Cain's offering was not accepted. So Cain became very angry. Have you ever had that feeling where it seems you just can't get anything right? That was Cain's position right now. He's frustrated and downcast.

God came to correct him but he wouldn't listen, so he left God's presence.

By the end of verse eight, Cain had killed his brother. God came right there again and asked him about Abel, and Cain answered in sarcasm.

Read the story for yourself and let's examine a few lessons.

1. What does God want?

From the very beginning of history, man has always desired acceptance. Something built into every one of us that craves approval. We want the approval of our parents, we want it from friends, and from society. But what does it take to earn the respect of God?

This is not about favouritism. God doesn't play favourites, rather it is about approval when someone has done something right. We learn in the book of Hebrews that Abel gave his offerings by faith and "Without faith, it is impossible to please God."

What does this mean?

How many times have you done something just because you were required to do it? Or like we say, 'to fulfill righteousness.' Such actions have no rewards or positive results. Whatever you do, do it with all your heart and a true sense of commitment.

Abel offered a more acceptable sacrifice and this he did, by faith. Heartless religion and repetition are a waste of time. If you do things just for the sake of it, it brings no reward.

When you pick your books to read, are you really interested in reading or do you simply want to show your parents that you're reading - you are obeying the instruction but your heart is not there.

When you have homework to do, do you take time to do some study? Or you simply hope to copy someone else's notes on Monday morning. There may not be immediate consequences to your choices but don't get mad when those who put in the heart receive the rewards of their diligence.

So when next you go to church or you give an offering, do it with all your heart and God will have respect for you and He will accept your gifts.

This lesson also extends to business and creativity. When you decide to bring your work to the marketplace, realize that there is an existing standard that the market requires. Make every effort to bring excellence to the table and your value will be respected.

Money is an exchange you receive for the value you bring. Don't just do your best, do the best. Be the best, and keep improving yourself. The market will not reduce its standards to accommodate you. Find out what your competition is doing better than you and strive to close that gap and even exceed it.

God said to Cain, "If you do the right thing, you will be accepted." That was Cain's chance to correct himself but he blew it.

Don't blow your chance. Do the right thing.

2. Deconstructing Envy

Once upon a time, in the story of Jesus, A woman named Mary Magdalene had come to anoint Jesus with a very costly perfume. The people present began to murmur and complain, but in the midst of that, Judas spoke up. He said, "Why this waste? This perfume could have been sold at a high price, and the money given to the poor."

The bible records that Judas' statement was not because he cared for the poor. He was a thief. The bible also records that, after this event, Judas went to the chief priest to betray Jesus.

Dear Abel, beware of your brother, Cain.

Cain is a picture of that jealous brother or your so-called friend. Do not be naive. Not everyone who calls you 'friend' should be your friend. If they criticize you in public, they are not your friend. When you have a public victory and everyone is celebrating, beware of your so-called friend who would not celebrate in public but sends you a private message.

If they fail to acknowledge and affirm your strengths, they are not your friend. If they do not wholeheartedly rejoice with you in your victories, you should be careful. They are silent when you win, but quickly offer words of encouragement when you fail. They never discuss your plans for future success. They are always encouraging you to pick up fights with other people.

Abel should have noticed Cain's mood. He had a frown on his face and God noticed. Abel would have known when Cain said to him, "Let us go out to the field." He didn't return from that journey.

A word for Cain on this one:

Why exactly are you angry Cain? If Abel's offering was rejected, would you still be angry? Selah.

3. Sin always finds you out.

Cain was angry because Abel's offering got accepted and his was not. Cain was angry but he had not sinned yet. Do you remember the scripture that says, "Be angry and sin not." It is possible.

So Cain was angry but he was also jealous. He was jealous of Abel. But God wanted to accept Cain so he called out to him with correction and advice. "If you do well," God said. "Will you not be accepted?"

Let's pause for a moment and revisit the first lesson about What God really wants. You should do your best to find out what the quality standards are. Whether it is about the quality of offerings, or quality of answers in an examination, or the quality of products/services that you bring to the marketplace. Decide what it is you want to achieve, find out what it will take to achieve it. Ensure that you do the best. Don't just do 'your best' do 'the best'

Cain didn't listen to that advice from God. So he let his anger and jealousy overtake him. He killed his brother Abel and buried him. Gross right? Yeah.

Here's something else to note. Even though Cain was jealous, killing Abel didn't get him accepted rather it earned him a curse. Putting other people down does not in any way lift you up. When you refuse to compliment other people, it doesn't make you look better. And sooner or later, what you did will find you out.

4. Cain, where is your brother?

The first thing to say here is, be your brother's keeper. Look out for those you care about - a friend, sibling, or colleague at work. Be kind. Moving on from there, this question is still valid to this day, and I ask you holding this book right now, where is your brother?

Abel is a picture of that brother, classmate, or friend who is doing better than you, in school or the neighbourhood. Everybody seems to like him. He seems to be daddy's favourite. Abel is a picture of that colleague in the office who is always getting the award as best performing staff of the year.

Dear young person, Abel is not your enemy. Abel is not your problem. He is not the reason why you are underperforming. Rather Abel should be your role model and a challenge for you to do better.

When you sit to binge on Netflix, where is your brother?

When you spend your little resources on gambling (or is it betting you call it), where is your brother?

When you choose to sleep an extra hour, where is your brother?

While you are hanging out in the club every weekend, Cain, where is your brother?

Abel is not your problem. Stop the blame game already. Take responsibility for your life and you will begin to change your outcomes.

5. Cain negotiates

Cain had just been found guilty of murder and a sentence has been passed on him. Strangely though, Cain is negotiating the terms of his judgment. This may sound strange to the very religious but hey, you can negotiate the outcomes of your own life if you do the right thing.

For starters you can confess your sin, repent and ask forgiveness.

You don't have to accept what is. If you are willing and obedient, you will eat the good of the land. We would learn more about this from another pair of teens - Jacob and Esau.

6. Social Media

Before the advent of social media, if your friend lived far away, you could not tell when he/she got a new dress or the expensive birthday party their parents threw during the holidays. You had no clue where they hung out and where they travelled to. Because of this, comparison was low and so was the need for inferiority and jealousy.

In today's era of instant messaging, everything and anything goes on the gram. One of the greatest undoing of the so-called Gen-Z is his/her flagrant disregard for privacy. There seems to be a competition for who will outdo the other in baring it all.

This culture feeds the problem of low self-esteem in young, rejection and in extreme cases, suicide amongst young people.

Here the Apostle Paul in 2 Corinthians 10:12,

"For we dare not class ourselves or compare ourselves with those who commend themselves. But they, measuring themselves by themselves, and comparing themselves among themselves, are not wise."

Abel, stop displaying all your life on social media. We do not need all that information, and you do not need that type of validation. Your identity and validation comes from God who lives on your inside. Besides, Cain might be watching you, he does not need to know.

Cain, stop comparing yourself with Abel. You are different and God loves you too. You may not get it right the first time, but if you keep working on yourself and getting better, your time will come.

Dear young person, stop the comparison. Seek to discover your true self, and stay on the pursuit of your personal development. Honour your destiny. You are different.

REVIEW QUESTIONS:

1. Which area of your life do you need to up your game?

   _____

   _____

   _____

   _____

2. How do you relate with people who are better than you?

   _____

   _____

   _____

   _____

3. Are there people you need to apologise to or things you need to apologise for?

   _____

   _____

   _____

   _____

4. Who should you be looking out for, going for?

   _____

   _____

   _____

   _____

NOTE TO PARENTS:

Don't always treat your children equally. Treat them with equity. What that means is Jay should not always get a toy simply because Kay got one.

You can only do that for so long. A time will come, and pretty soon, when you can no longer be the rescue. Then reality will have to be their new parent, and reality does not play 'fair'.

As early as possible, introduce merits, rewards, and consequences in your parenting plan. This is different from favouritism, and needs to be taught so the kids don't get the wrong message. Set standard and reward systems for tasks and assignments.

NOTES

2. JACOB AND ESAU - SIBLING SQUABBLES, AGAIN

Reference: Genesis 25-33

Sibling rivalry, again? Yes.

This story is a long one. It covers the entire lives of two brought from the time they were born right through their adulthood and even old age. But we will concern ourselves more with their life as youths.

Jacob and Esau were twin brothers born to the family of Isaac and Rebekah. From what we read, their squabbles began when they were in their mother's womb. Esau is the older guy and Jacob was second so the birthright belonged to Esau. As they grew older, Esau became a hunter while Jacob started to rear animals, a shepherd. Does this sound familiar?

Before we continue, let's take a step back and understand what birthright is.

The birthright is an honour usually given to the first son in the family. He would receive a double share of the father's inheritance. Birthright also comes with rights, privileges, and responsibilities. This birthright is transferred by an oral declaration of blessings.

So back to the story, Esau had the birthright because he was the firstborn. One day, Esau came back from his hunting trip hungry and tired. Then he decides to ask Jacob for relief - a plate of food, but

Jacob makes a bargain with his food and Esau trades the birthright with him.

Many years later, as their father was about to die, he calls for Esau to fulfill a requirement in order to get the blessing. At this point, their mom interferes and Jacob tricks Isaac into giving him the blessing. When Esau found out what happened, it was too late as the blessing cannot be reversed.

1. Value Systems

Let's begin our lessons from values. Jacob and Esau represent two value systems. Our values are a set of principles or standards by which we live. It is how we behave and decide what is important in life. In this story, we find two opposite value systems as chosen by the twins: one is focused on the short-term (now) while the other is focused on the long-term (later).

While Esau was thinking about the evening meal, Jacob had his eye on the future, the blessing of the birthright. Jacob was willing to go hungry for the night in order to get the blessing. Esau on the other hand was willing to give away the birthright in exchange for an evening meal. That meal represents an episode in your favourite TV series, it could be an evening with the boys or a girls' night out, it could be a match between your favourite sports teams, etc. Any of these in exchange for your future. The future is in those exams you have just registered for, or a job interview on Monday morning.

Actions have consequences, and the choices we make determine the rest of our lives. We decide our values, but our values decide our future. Choose wisely.

Some other values we see in this story include; planning, delayed gratification, discipline. While Esau was careless about that night, Jacob had a plan in mind. I think that Esau had been eating Jacob's food for free before that night. That night was different but he didn't realize it. Stop being careless with your life.

Jacob also practiced delayed gratification, something I think he developed as a farmer. Farmers understand planting and waiting for the harvest. Hunters on the other hand want the results immediately. So Jacob knew that just one night without food was capable of giving him a lifetime harvest of blessings.

2. Choices - A deal is a deal.

Have you ever been in a situation where you thought you didn't have a choice? Well, I guess Esau was in that situation. Here he was, tired from the day's work, no catch for the day, and he was hungry. He thought he had no choice. Then he also said "Look, I am about to die..." but he was not about to die, he was just hungry. The choice he had was the choice that Jacob took - to stay hungry for the night. So Esau chose to trade his prized possession for a meal.

It looks as though Esau did not understand the impact of what happened that night, because, many years later, he was going to prepare a meal for his dad as a requirement to receive the blessing. Did he forget the deal with Jacob? Or did he just think it didn't matter? Same for many of us, sometimes we think that the choices we make have no consequences or that it wouldn't matter much when the time comes. But every choice matters, some matter less than others though. For instance, whether you take a cold or hot shower; whether you use a black or a blue pouch. Things like that have little or no consequence to your future, but many of the choices we make every day have real consequences.

The friends we hang out with, the value systems we choose, the eating habits we pick up, our taste in fashion, whether to read or see a movie, the options we make in our course of study, etc. All these have very serious consequences on how we turn out in life. Our lives are governed by the philosophies we choose to live by.

There is always a choice to make, and we are responsible for our choices. We make our choice, then our choices make us.

3. The Deal.

Esau! What did you just sign?

We have established that Esau wasn't thinking long-term when he agreed to Jacob's deal. Esau is shortsighted. Esau is the kind of guy that agrees to anything that looks good without really thinking about the consequences of his action. But in these times of "terms and conditions", do not just sign every contract you receive.

This applies to every field of business, but I have seen it more with young people who are starting their careers in entertainment, sports, or those in the modeling industry. Always enter a business deal with clearly written agreements. Ensure that you have read every clause in the agreement before you sign it. If in doubt, get expert advice. Seek counsel from a mentor, coach, lawyer, or professional in the field you're going to venture into.

Do not sign that document until you understand the language and meaning of the document. This is because words mean different things in different professions and industries, and that is why you need professional advice. Look before you leap, they say. I'd say, read, understand before you sign. Experience is the best teacher when you are learning from the experiences of other people.

4. You can start today.

In Chapter x, we learnt from the story of Cain and Abel that you can renegotiate your destiny. You don't have to take what is given.

We see that again in this story. After Isaac had blessed Jacob and Esau wept for the blessing he had just missed, Isaac added a caveat in what seemed like a cause on Jacob. He said, "But when you grow restless, you will throw his yoke from off your neck."

In that sentence lies Esau's escape from the curse. You may have made a mess of your life up to this point, but you can make a reverse, start today to redesign your life for good. A few things you would require include;

Repentance: You must acknowledge that you messed up. You were wrong, and you have to be sorry for that. Ask God for forgiveness, He himself said He is faithful and just to forgive. There may be people you have wronged also. Apologise and make peace with them.

Skill: You must be willing to refine your God-given abilities into marketable skills, but this requires the third ingredient;

Your will: You must be ready to apply yourself to the process of change. If you are WILLING and OBEDIENT, you will eat the good of the land (See Isaiah 1:19). Success in any area follows a set of laws that you must obey. Don't just wish for it, you must apply your will to it.

Sure, the blessing does give you an edge, but it does not exempt you from the work. Diligence is a choice you must make if you desire to be successful. I call it "Godly restlessness." You have to be ready to go to work. You have to wake up early for school. You must spend time studying. You must take the exams and pass if you want a seat at the table of success.

Many people of faith, especially from this part of the world are, in fact, lazy. They think that the blessing is all you need to become a success. We would rather pray than read. We would rather go to mountains and camps seeking miracle money than work at a job or business. There is this weird sense of grace that we have and I hope that you reading this now would dare to be different.

Here this from the mouth of one of the most successful bible characters, "But by the grace of God I am what I am, and his grace to me was not without effect. No, I worked harder than all of them— yet not I, but the grace of God that was with me."

Dear young person, let the grace of God push you to work because faith without works is dead.

When Esau learnt this lesson, he too became a wealthy man. One time Jacob was on a journey and met Esau on the way. Jacob feared for his life and decided to send gifts to Esau in order to make peace. They made peace, but Esau looked at his gifts and said, "I have enough, my brother; keep what you have for yourself."

5. Hard work alone will not be enough.

In this story, Jacob is used to hard work, wit, and wisdom, or street smart. Remember that even from the womb, he grabbed his brother by the heel. Then he traded for the birthright, then he had that encounter with his uncle while he was running from Esau (Genesis 29-31), and by this time he was already a grown man. This guy is used to being smart but smart has made him enemies everywhere. But of what use is success when you are always looking above your shoulders in fear.

So Jacob makes a decision to find God's favour. He prayed all night, and we are told he wrestled with an angel. It was after this event that he made peace with Esau. Work hard. Also, seek the grace of God in your life. The grace of God will give you favour with people, and favour is a currency that you need for success.

REVIEW QUESTIONS:

1. What are your personal values?

_____

_____

_____

_____

2. Jacob had his stew. What do you have that you can use to negotiate for your future?

_____

_____

_____

3. Have you ever had to give up something important for something less valuable?

_____

_____

_____

_____

4. How can you apply the lessons from this story in your life?

_____

_____

_____

_____

NOTE TO PARENTS:

The Jacob and Esau story reveals a faulty parenting style adopted by Isaac and Rebekah. Both already had favourites among the twins. Isaac chose Esau whereas Rebekah favoured Jacob.

If both parents were equally involved in the lives of the twins, things would have been different.

NOTES

3. JOSEPH - FROM GRASS TO GRACE

Reference: Genesis 37, 39-50

Joseph's is a grass-to-grace story with everything else in-between. The story begins in Genesis 37 and runs like a movie series down to chapter 50. Of course, some of it covered his adult life. It starts from when he was 17 years old and follows through for 20 years at which time, he was 37.

Joseph was the son of Jacob and Rachel. His father had two wives and 12 sons. Joseph was the 11th son with one brother from his mom and 10 other half-brothers. His brothers hated him because he was daddy's favourite, and their dad, Jacob, made a coat of many colours, specially for Joseph.

At 17, Joseph had a dream in which he was a ruler and his brothers and parents came to bow before him. He shared this dream with the family and his brothers hated him the more for it. This hatred caused them to sell him into slavery. They really wanted him dead, but Reuben suggested the option of selling him instead. They dipped his coat in animal blood to convince their father that he had been killed by a wild animal.

Joseph got sold twice and ended up in the house of Potiphar, a senior officer in Pharaoh's secret service, in faraway Egypt (Pharaoh is the title of the King in ancient Egypt). Potiphar put

Joseph in charge of his household because he was exceptional. Not long after, Mrs. Potiphar started to crush on Joseph so she began to seduce him, but Joseph would not agree. On one occasion, she tried to force herself on Joseph but he ran away leaving his shirt with her.

Mrs. Potiphar is angry with Joseph for rejecting her advances, she lied against him and got him sent to jail.

While in prison, Joseph found favour before the authorities and he was again put in charge of other inmates. In his prison cell were two officials of Pharaoh's palace, and one night, they both had dreams and asked Joseph to interpret their dreams. Joseph's interpretation came to pass and one of the officials was set free while the other was sentenced to death.

Two years later, Pharaoh had a dream that troubled him and needed an interpreter. That was when the official from Joseph's cell remembered Joseph. Joseph came to the limelight by interpreting Pharaoh's dream as he was appointed Prime Minister of Egypt.

Let's take a closer look to find what we can learn from this Old Testament picture of Jesus - yes, I'll tell you how.

1. A Type of Jesus.

Joseph is his father's favourite son whom he sent to check on his brothers but they sold him as a slave. Jesus (God's only begotten) was loved by the father and sent to his brothers - the Israelites, some accepted him but the majority rejected and hated him. Jesus was betrayed by the one closest to him and, like Joseph, he was sold for silver pieces.

Joseph was thrown into a pit (cistern) just before he went to Egypt. Jesus was buried in a tomb, and he too came out. A robe was put on him which his killers made a mockery of.

Like Jesus, Joseph was accused of the things he didn't do and sent to prison. While in prison, he meets two guys, one dies and the other meets him in the palace. Remember the two thieves at the cross of Jesus and the promise of paradise to one of them? Both after 3 days.

The baker makes bread while the butler bears wine. Bread and wine are two elements of the Holy Communion which Jesus introduced to his disciples.

Joseph's first robe was taken from him and smeared with blood. The same happened to Jesus when they cast lots with his robe. But in Genesis 41, Joseph is given another robe by the king of Egypt. Revelations 19 says that Jesus will return with a robe marked, "King of kings and Lord of lords."

It's not the same story but don't miss the connection. In the end, God can take an entirely messed up story and turn it into a blockbuster. He did it with Joseph. He did it with Jesus. God can do it with your life as well.

2. Purpose Discovery.

We begin with a lesson on purpose. Now I'm sure you've heard those words before, but what is it exactly? It is the seed in your heart that springs up like a vision, a dream, and an aspiration. Usually, it will involve other people.

In the form of a dream, Joseph's purpose started to call out to him at the age of seventeen. He didn't quite understand it so he shared this dream with his brothers, and with his parents.

Your purpose is not something you fabricate, it is something you discover. And discovery takes time, lots of careful inquiry, and patience. Now there are a number of things required for you to discover and clarify your purpose, but I'm going to ask you to begin with prayer. If you believe that God made you, then He must have the manual for the product He made.

God will give you a vision for your life, but there is no fixed pattern for this discovery. When you make the discovery, it will be your responsibility to also find the path for the fulfillment of that vision.

3. Discretion.

Joseph shared this dream with his brothers, and with his parents. They hated him more because of his dream and because of what he said. God has big plans for you but you have to learn to deal with the real world. It may be better to keep your dreams to yourself. Just be careful and use wise discretion.

The book of Proverbs has this for you: "Discretion will preserve you; Understanding will keep you, to deliver you from the way of evil, from the man who speaks perverse things, from those who leave the paths of uprightness To walk in the ways of darkness;" (Proverbs 2:11-13).

In the dreams of Joseph, his brothers are humbled but that humbling is God's plan to save their lives. Before Joseph is exalted, he too will be humbled.

If you sense that God has big plans for you, get ready to be humbled. Every bible hero went through this process - Moses, Elisha, David, Daniel, Jesus, and all his disciples, and in fact, every hero you can think of.

This brings us again to the subject of dealing with rejection. Don't expect everyone to like you or to accept your big dreams. Remember what we learnt? Manage your expectations wisely.

4. Character / Discipline / Purity.

There's a lot to say about Joseph's character, but let's discuss a few. In chapter 37 of Genesis, Joseph quickly went from being his father's favourite son to being sold into slavery (Remember the Jesus connection - from God's only begotten to being born in a manger). Then by the beginning of chapter 39, he is already a slave in Potiphar's house.

The bible doesn't tell us anything about Joseph's trauma. It seems he wasn't one to dwell on the negative sides of his life – one who wouldn't wallow in self-pity. Joseph went to work in this new environment where he found himself and he excelled.

This is not to say that he didn't feel the pain, the betrayal, and rejection, the loneliness of being separated from his family. We see that in his reactions at the end of the story, but Joseph exhibited the strength of his character in focusing on the present and making the most of it.

17-year-old Joseph is hard-working, industrious, and diligent. This earned him a place of leadership in Potiphar's house as well as in prison. Remember, this is not some ugly guy. Joseph was "well-built and handsome." He is a cool dude.

It was his good looks and good character that got him into his next trouble. Let this remind you that there are challenges that come with being physically attractive. And yes, sometimes being good can get you in trouble, and that's okay too.

Here comes the temptation, and dilemma. Mrs. Potiphar will kill you if you say no to her, but Potiphar will kill you if you say yes. Either way, you die so you have to choose which death you prefer. Joseph is young and single. I mean, he could take his chance on this one but the stakes are high, and Joseph knows what's at stake here. His position in the boss' house, his relationship with the boss and with God, his dreams, his family, his destiny, his life. There's a lot on the line, beyond the few minutes of 'fun' with Mrs. Potiphar.

When you face temptations as we all do, do you stop to consider what is at stake? Usually, Mrs. Potiphar would have nothing to lose, and here's a lesson I learnt long ago: never do business with someone who has little or nothing to lose.

Some of the biggest names in bible history are made or marred by sexual temptation - Samson, David, Solomon are examples. That 5 minutes can alter the course of your life forever.

Notice also that this was not a one-time encounter. Mrs. Potiphar persisted with her asking and Joseph persisted with his refusal until that moment when Mrs. Potiphar went from just asking, to taking it by force. Joseph fled. Many times, temptation doesn't leave you alone simply because you said 'No.' It will try again and again. Like Joseph, you have to run. Joseph understood the power of discipline and delayed gratification to achieve a greater result in the future. Do not be deceived by pleasure and the promise of immediate rewards

All through the story, we read that, "The Lord was with Joseph." Therein lies one of the main secrets for Joseph's victory - The Lord was with him. You too can get the Lord on your side.

5. Gifts, Talents, Skill. Diligence.

This part is in chapter 40 of the book of Genesis. Two of Pharaoh's officers offended their boss and were sent to prison, in the same prison where Joseph is in charge. Both of them had a dream and were sad because they couldn't interpret their dreams. Joseph comes along and declares that the interpretation of dreams belonged to God. Looks like Joseph can hardly have a conversation without bringing God into it. And that's a lesson for us. Remember what we said about the Lord being with Joseph. Joseph acknowledges God every step of the way and for the gifts and talents that he has, even the gift of interpretation of dreams. This approach is what determined how Joseph responded to all the issues in his life.

So in the course of interpreting these two men's dreams, Joseph makes a request to the one with the good dream, "When all goes well with you, remember me." Here, Joseph is using his skill to negotiate his freedom. In the midst of hard times, and when it looks like all hope is lost, always remember your gifts and talents. You should spend time to develop those gifts into skills, they'll come in handy one day. That was David's strategy, and now Joseph. It could be yours too.

In the midst of this though, the bottler forgot about Joseph for two years. Those to whom you have been goodwill not always remember, do good anyway. It pays.

After "two full years." Sometimes you need to wait that long for your dreams to come true and for the manifestation of God's plan. Diligence requires time and effort to prove. Your dreams are valid but they will come at a price, and not overnight. The price is discipline, diligence, and work. So after two years, Pharaoh had a distressing dream, and that's when the butler remembered.

Again, Joseph drags God into the equation. He said, "I cannot do it, but God will give Pharaoh the answer he desires." God honoured Joseph's humility.

Pharaoh's dream was a matter of national importance, and Joseph proffers the solution. He put together an economic master plan for the president. Take note that by this time, Joseph is already 30 years old so what started in teen life leads into his 30s. He has been honing his leadership skills from home, to Potiphar's house, and to prison. Everything you're doing today is leading you directly into your adult life. Be careful. You may one day be required to lead a nation or to come up with a plan for a company where you work. Will you be ready?

Joseph was ready and Pharaoh, after listening to his pitch, made the declaration that changed Joseph's life forever. From slave to a prisoner, and now prime minister, of the world's superpower at that time and one of the greatest nations in history. Wow!

6. Joseph's Brothers

A bit about these guys. It's easy for us to want to be Joseph in this story but in reality, some, if not most of us are more of his brothers than Joseph. These guys lived a lie for 20 whole years.

Famine hit and they had to travel to Egypt for food, but not just for food. Unknown to them, they came face to face with their 20-year-old deception.

Sin will always find you out. Remember Cain. And it is virtually impossible to commit just one sin.

These brothers started by being envious. Envy led to (attempted) murder and that led to the lie they told their father. Imagine how much it must have taken them to maintain this lie for 20 whole years before the truth came out.

But with that lie came the guilt. 20 years later their guilt follows them as we see in their journey to and from Egypt before the reconciliation. Not only were they guilty all this while, getting rid of Joseph still didn't earn them the love of their father.

7. Forgiveness.

The journey of reconciliation begins in chapter 42 and runs through to 45. Your life is a journey and if you have chosen the wrong direction, you will need to retrace your steps. But it's not that easy in real life. First, you must acknowledge where you missed it and be willing to do what it takes.

If you have hurt someone, there is a lesson from the life of Joseph's brothers - Judah particularly (Read Genesis 44). It was Judah who started to take responsibility, having realized their sins. He suggested the idea of selling Joseph, but now, he is willing to give himself in order to save Benjamin. There's only one way to find forgiveness, it is repentance.

For the one who is hurting. You must learn to trust God with your emotions and lean on him for help. Imagine the hurt from 20 years ago, and how Joseph handled the situation. "You intended to harm me, but God intended it for good to accomplish what is now being done, the saving of many lives." That is not an easy thing to say, but for the man who has always known and trusted God all his life, it is as simple as that.

There is also the case of Mrs. Potiphar. Joseph was wrongly accused and sentenced to prison by the lustful actions of Mrs. Potiphar, and of course, Mr. Potiphar believed his wife. Joseph would have been justified to use his new position as Governor and Prime Minister of Egypt to punish the sins of Potiphar and his wife. That was a case of attempted rape, wrong accusation and defamation of character. He spent two years in jail. Contrary to what many others would have done, there was never a mention of this case again, and in the other of government, Potiphar continued to enjoy his position under Joseph.

Forgiveness is the only weapon you have, to deal with the grudge in your heart. If you like Joseph, decide to look over your story and see God through it all, you will realize, like he did, that God can work his purpose into all of your experiences.

There it is, the story of Joseph. I hope you've found it as interesting as I did. Let's move on now.

REVIEW QUESTIONS:

1. Can you describe a vision you have about your future?

_____

_____

_____

_____

2. How can you be a blessing to the people in your life?

_____

_____

_____

_____

3. What gifts/talents did Joseph have? What about you?

_____

_____

_____

_____

4. How else can you apply the lessons from Joseph's story?

_____

_____

_____

_____

NOTE TO PARENTS:

On Envy:

Envy is destructive. It destroys relationships and generations. This particular envy is caused by the parent's favouritism. One would think that Jacob should have known better, having been a victim of his father's favouritism, but apparently, he didn't learn that lesson.

Favouritism damages all the children, including the favoured ones.

Jacob set up his favoured son against the others. It's bad enough that Joseph wouldn't go to work with his elder brothers (maybe for good reason), but then Jacob sent him to go check on them. It appears that Jacob encouraged the behaviour of Joseph to report his siblings to their father. This was the first reason the brothers hated Joseph.

Dear Parents, I believe young people call it 'snitching'. Do not set your child up to snitch on their siblings. Children will have enough reasons to fight amongst themselves, don't be the enabler of the fight.

On Sibling Rivalry:

There's a good number of bible stories from sibling rivalry. Jacob deceived his father, Isaac, to get the blessing. Now his 10 sons deceive him to kill their brother.

Isaac quarreled with his brother, Ishmael. This time, one of Isaac's descendants is sold into slavery to the Ishmaelites (Ishmael's descendants).

Parents will do well to save generations by how we raise our kids and teach them to settle disputes amongst themselves.

NOTES

NOTES

4. DAVID - A YOUNG MAN AFTER GOD'S HEART

Reference: 1 Samuel 16-19

David is introduced in the bible as a shepherd boy tending his father's sheep somewhere in the fields. That was when God through the prophet Samuel anointed him as King. Then we learn about his music skills when he was invited to the palace to play for King Saul. This skill was developed while he was in the fields with sheep. As the sheep would graze, young David had enough time to practice his instruments and writing.

David's prominence eventually came when he defeated Israel's enemy, a giant named Goliath. This feat brought him closer to the king and he became a favourite friend of the king's son, Jonathan. He also got recruited into the army as one of Israel's soldiers.

Later in the story, King Saul feels threatened by David's prominence; Saul saw David as wanting to take his crown. For this reason, Saul planned to kill David.

The story of David is a very interesting one and arguably the most popular bible character story. He made some mistakes as a boy and as a king, and God made him receive the consequences of those mistakes.

In the end, Saul and his son Jonathan die in a war and David is chosen as king.

The bible does not state exactly how old David was but here's what we know; David was a boy when he was anointed by the Prophet Samuel, and since he was old enough to be left in charge of the sheep, that would put him somewhere around 12 years of age. And by the time he confronted Goliath, he was not yet in the army. The official age for joining the army at that time was age 20, so we can tell that David was not older than 19 years of age. But by the time he became king, it is on record that he was 30 years old. This would give us an idea of the timeline of events in David's life.

1. Hard work.

From his introduction in 1Sam 16, it appears that David's job was unpleasant, at least to the rest of the family.

However, there is no doubt that David was a hardworking young man. David was not an idle person. As a teenager, he was already responsible for the family business of animal husbandry.

The Bible describes David as handsome and good-looking, with bright/beautiful eyes. He was the lastborn with seven older brothers. Yet this fine boy, young as he was, was alone in the field saddled with the responsibility of taking care of his father's flock of sheep.

Out there in the fields, think about all the dangers he was exposed to.

Dear young person, you are not too young to work. You are not too young to take some responsibility, in the home and for yourself. It is not too early to get involved in daddy and mummy's business. You're not too young to learn how things work and how to handle business operations.

You are involved. Get involved.

2. Dealing with Rejection 1Sa 16:1-10

David was the left-behind kid. The one that no one remembered. Remember that his father did not mention his name when the prophet inquired about the sons of Jesse.

This might be you. You may have been rejected by those whose acceptance you value. This could be a group of school/classmates who you admire; it may be a boy or girl that you are attracted to but they don't like you in return, or maybe a teacher at school who is not very friendly with you as with others.

Manage your expectations from people. Take a course on Personal Identity and Self-Esteem. Your friends may exclude you or leave you behind in certain conversations. Some people will not recognize you. That's their business, not yours. Mind your own business. Manage your expectations wisely and be at peace with everyone.

You may even feel like your parents love your siblings more than they love you. Young David experienced that too. Yet, he went on to become the most celebrated king in the history of his nation.

Think about that and let it give you the courage to love yourself regardless of what others think of you.

'But Uncle D, it's hard.' I know but it's not impossible. Oftentimes the path to kingship is lonely. Peace does not mean you accept their behaviour but you honour your destiny so much that you pay no mind to your naysayers.

Make excuses for them. If they know better, they will probably do better.

3. Developing Skill. 1Sa 16:18-23

David was a great musician in his time. He could play the instruments so well and he was a great writer and composer. He wrote 75% of the entire book of psalms. He is called the sweet psalmist of Israel. I like to think of young David as a great high-life musician or the king of pop in his generation.

In the fields where David spent most of his time, he found it a good place to fellowship with God. He played the harp and wrote his own songs, some of those songs were prayers while others were worship songs. David kept a record of these writings and that is how we have the book of Psalms today. That book is probably the most popular and most-read book of the bible.

He did not only write, but he also played the instrument. Some say his music was also a tool for gathering his flock. Over time, David perfected his musical skills and could play skillfully and excellently to the point that his music could cast out demons and heal the sick. David was a music therapist.

One time the king of Israel, King Saul was sick. He had a mental illness which also caused him depression and insomnia. This illness we are told was caused by evil spirits. The king's servants became very concerned and they needed to get therapy for the king. They needed to find a good musician who could play the harp. Someone immediately recommended David and he got the job.

The servant that recommended David must have heard him play in the past, and David must have done a good job then. In Proverbs 22:29, the bible says, "Do you see a man diligent *and skillful* in his business? He will stand before kings; he will not stand before obscure men." APMC

4. Skill, Mastery, Courage. 1Sa 17

Ancient Palestine had been Israel's greatest enemy (I think they still are, even today). About 3,000 years ago, Israel was attacked by Palestine. Both armies were stuck on two mountains facing each other with a valley between them and none would dare to attack first.

To break the tie, the Palestinians sent forward their mightiest warrior to challenge the nation of Israel to a duel. The duel was a strategy used in ancient history for settling wars to avoid large casualties.

This guy is about 9ft tall, broad, his armour alone weighs a hundred and fifty pounds (70kg) not to mention his heavy javelin, sword, and shield. He was massive. Then he had a loudmouth. He bragged about how he had killed Israel's soldiers and his many feats in the past. He threatened and cursed out the Israeli soldiers but they were all too afraid to meet him for a fight.

Then comes David, the shepherd boy. His father, Jesse had sent him to check on his brothers who were on the battlefront. He hears the rumours about a certain giant that no one is willing to fight. First, David wants to know, "What shall be done for the man who kills this Philistine and takes away the reproach from Israel?"

For speaking up, and asking a harmless question David's eldest brother accused him of arrogance and of neglecting their father and his sheep. Remember what we learnt about dealing with rejection. David ignored him and went on to ask other people.

A lifetime tax exemption for him and his family; a chance to marry the princess (which would make him a prince), etc. Not only was the offer good, but it would also bring David closer to fulfilling destiny having been anointed king. So he was fighting for destiny. David also understood that God's honour was at stake. *You should always be clear about what you are fighting for. Every battle (quarrels, social media wars, and trends) is not for you. Some of the things that young people spend their time on are only a waste of time.*

The next hurdle to cross was the hurdle of Saul's approval. "You are just a youth," Saul said. "This man (Goliath) has been fighting since his youth." This speaks to Goliath's experience. David also had to recall his own experiences, killing a bear and a lion while taking care of his father's sheep. Think about that for a moment.

If you read the story, David ended up killing this giant with a sling and stone. So it appears that while David was out there in the field with his sheep, he didn't just master the art of writing and making music, he also spent time developing his ability to use the sling. In the book of Judges, a story is told about some soldiers who could use the sling so well, they could shoot at a hair strand and not miss (Judges 20:16). Those guys were from Benjamin's tribe and David was not from that tribe. However, it appears that David learnt this skill and developed himself so well that he was the one who saved the day in favour of his nation.

Goliath was a giant, alright, but giants are not as strong as they seem if only you can discover your strengths and skills. David had faith in God but his faith had to be deployed via the skill and experience which he had proven over time. The greatest impact our lives can have isn't in the moment where greatness begins: it's what happens before that moment.

5. David and Jonathan

One of the key ingredients in David's success story was his friendship with Jonathan. David and Jonathan got connected after the victory over Goliath, and the quickly became friends.

If you're going to become king, who better to make friends with than the son of a king? Choose your friends in line with the purpose you have discovered for your life. In being friends with Jonathan, David would have learnt how to think and act like a king. David would have learnt how to lead a nation, including how to build and lead an army. At the time of defeating Goliath, David was alone, but by the time he became king, David had raised a team known as "David's Mighty Men."

The relationship between David and Jonathan is one that teaches honour and loyalty. Jonathan was willing to submit to the gifts he had seen in David. Even though he was Crown Prince, he recognized the hand of God on his friend and honours that calling. Your true friends are those who are not threatened by the greatness of your vision and ideas.

REVIEW QUESTIONS:

1. What talents or strengths do you have?

_____

_____

_____

_____

2. How can you develop that talent into a skill?

_____

_____

_____

_____

3. What qualities of a friend can we find in Jonathan?

_____

_____

_____

_____

4. What else can you learn from David's story?

_____

_____

_____

_____

NOTE TO PARENTS:

Encourage hard work using simple tasks at home. Do not always try to save your child from every little difficulty. Let your teenagers engage in activities that build and develop grit.

There might be some experiences in the life of a young person that make them feel excluded or rejected. Use affirmations to build a positive self-image and esteem.

Use the family time to ask questions and help young people identify their strengths, encourage exploration of different interests, and provide avenues for honing these interests into skills. This is a three-step process of discovery, development, and deployment.

NOTES

NOTES

5. JOSIAH - THE LAST OF THE GOOD KINGS

Reference: 2 Kings 22-23, 2 Chronicles 34-36

Josiah is popularly referred to as the last good king in Israel. He became the King of Judah (the two southern tribes of Israel) at the age of eight from what was a lineage of evil kings. His father and grandfather, King Amon and King Manasseh were both known for their wickedness in leading the people of Judah.

"He did that which was right in the sight of the Lord, and walked in all the way of David his father."

Josiah defied the impact of his negative upbringing and earned an honourable reputation for himself.

Let's see what we can learn from this young leader.

1. Leadership

We are not told about the early years of his reign most likely because he was still a child. It appears that Josiah sought the help of some older men in Israel to enable him to lead the nation.

Asking for help is not weakness, it is a sign of humility, wisdom, and strength. Successful people understand that they need help to be successful.

Then Josiah picks his role models. He chose to follow the example of previous good kings in Israel. These include kings like Jehoshaphat, Hezekiah, and David. Whatever you are trying to do, someone has done before. Look back in history, find your role models and study their paths. In those stories lie the secrets of your success.

Also look at contemporary leaders in your time. Connect with them as much as you can. Do this without losing your identity. Whatever you learn can be added to your own voice to create a unique mix that is you.

2. Devotion

You are not too young to seek God.

"...in the eighth year of his reign, while he was still young, he began to seek the God of his father David;"

In the eighth year, Josiah would have been 16 years old. WHILE HE WAS STILL YOUNG, he sought God. Your teenage years are not a time to rebel against your parents and other authorities in your life. It is rather a good time to get serious with your life, and to seek God.

Do you have a relationship with God or you are simply doing what your parents have done. Are you seeking God or are you checking off a list of to-dos.

King Solomon has a piece of advice for us here. He said, "Remember now your Creator in the days of your youth, before the difficult days come, And the years draw near when you say, "I have no pleasure in them"" (Ecclesiastes 12:1

But if you choose to do otherwise, here's what the wise king says;

"Young people, enjoy yourselves while you are young; be happy [let your heart be merry] while you are young. Do whatever your heart desires [Follow the ways of your heart], whatever you want to do [follow the ways of your heart and the sight of your eyes]. But remember [know] that God will judge you for everything you do."

Ecclesiastes 11:9 (EXB)

It is more interesting to seek God and pursue purpose while you are young rather than old. Why throw away your best years on irrelevant pursuits? Be wise.

3. Humility and Discipline.

In the course of repairing the temple, Josiah makes a discovery of a document thought to have been lost. This document contained the laws and will of God for the nation of Israel. When the document was read to him, he became sober, but also decided to take action on what he had just heard.

What do you do when you realize what is right?

It is easier to cry early before you get beaten by life. The pain of discipline is always less than the pain of regret. The pain of personal repentance is often better than the pain of God's judgement.

Josiah was humbled and God took note of that and spared him from the calamity that was to come. God responds to humility, and brokenness. Life responds to diligence and discipline.

3. Choose the right team.

When he made the decision about the reformation, Josiah put men in charge of repairing the temple. There is a long list of names of people that helped Josiah accomplish his goals - prophets, priests, craftsmen, etc.

Leaders don't work alone, they know how to hire a great team. Same goes for personal leadership, you need to have the right kind of people in your friend's list if you desire to please God and to live a great life.

In business or your personal life, you retain the right to choose your circle.

4. Don't live for your past.

Many young people today have experiences of being raised in the most uncomfortable environments - Troubled homes, difficult neighbourhoods, etc. with little or no examples of good leadership, but good still triumphs over evil. The grace of God is still superior to your upbringing and with the right combination of your will, wit, godly wisdom, and grace, a person can override their heredity in fulfilling purpose.

Josiah was raised by an evil father, but ended up building a great reputation for himself, before men and before God.

REVIEW QUESTIONS:

1. What is your goal in life?

2. Do you have a responsive heart? When you are corrected, do you receive it with humility or throw it off in pride?

3. Will you take action on the things you hear or will you continue business as usual?

4. How will you apply the lessons from Josiah's story?

NOTE TO PARENTS:

Like Josiah, we all have an opportunity to do what is right irrespective of our past and backgrounds. Be willing to correct your mistakes and teach your children to do the same.

By all means, heal from your own hurts. You have heard the saying, "Hurting people hurt other people." Heal from your hurts so your children would not have to heal from you.

Do not continue to recycle pain. Get help.

NOTES

NOTES

6. ESTHER — QUEEN HADASSAH

Reference: The Book of Esther

Before we get into the Esther story, let us examine the background and everything that leads up to the emergence of a role model called Esther.

Around 2,500 years ago, Many Israelites were in exile spread across the entire Persian Empire which is in present-day Iran. The temple in Israel had just been rebuilt after being invaded by Babylon, but only a few persons have returned (part of this story is recorded in the book of Ezra and Nehemiah). The first king of this empire, named Darius has died and his son, Xerxes, is now in power. Darius lost in a battle with the Athenians and Xerxes was determined to make them pay for killing his father.

Xerxes is getting ready to invade Greece in a bid to avenge the death of his father. So as part of a plan to make sure he is not defeated, Xerxes is hosting a party to gain new allies and support for his invasion. This party is a display of wealth, splendour, and glory, it lasted for over 180 days (imagine a 6-month-long party).

It was at this party that King Xerxes gave a command for his wife, Queen Vashti, to join the parade. He wants to show off his wife too. Mind you that at this point, the king was drunk. Queen Vashti turned down his command and this got the king really upset. King Xerxes governs a region of 127 provinces and commands an army of over a million soldiers. He holds a big office and a big ego too. For six months, he had been trying to impress people at his party, so he wouldn't take the disrespect to his command lightly.

Xerxes asks his commanders for advice on what to do, and they too have their egos to protect, so they come up with a decision to dethrone the queen.

Queen Vashti probably had good reason to refuse the king's command. Coming to show herself in a parade before a bunch of drunk men was inappropriate and immoral. But in a culture where the king's command was law, she paid the price with her position as queen.

You cannot be a true leader if you are led by your ego. True respect and honour cannot be forced. This nation is seemingly strong but in reality, it is governed by emotionally weak, and insecure men. Power and wealth do not really offer healing for the soul.

Moving on now, three years later, Xerxes lost the war when he attacked Greece, and here he is without a wife. Then his personal aides suggested a beauty pageant to select Miss Persia who would become the new wife of the king and queen of Persia.

There you go, that is the backstory, and now we enter Esther.

One of the exiled Jews staying in the city at that time was Mordecai. This Mordecai had a little cousin named Hadassah (also known as Esther). Following the king's command for a beauty pageant, Esther was taken into the courts of the king to participate in the contest.

Esther found favour before the official in charge of the contest. This contest lasted an entire year (inclusive of beauty treatments and makeup), she progressed fast, winning the favour of other officials. Eventually, Esther came out tops and became Queen.

Note that, up to this point, Esther's true identity as a Jew is hidden from everyone else as advised by Mordecai.

In chapter 2 of the book of Esther, we are told that Mordecai uncovered a plot to kill King Xerxes. He passed this intel to the king through Queen Esther and thereby saved the king's life, but nothing else is said about him. His position was at the king's gate though it seems he was a representative of the Jews in the city.

Then comes Haman, the villain of this story. We are not told why, but Haman received a promotion to a very prominent position more like the prime minister of Persia. And a decree was passed for everyone to bow before him whenever he came around, but Mordecai would not.

A bit of backstory on Haman. He is a descendant of the Amalekite King Agag. The nation of Israel defeated the Amalekites in a war, many years ago (See 1 Samuel 15). So, as expected, Haman is not going to take lightly the disobedience of Mordecai.

It would have been okay to punish Mordecai for his disobedience, but Haman saw this as an opportunity to avenge a generational grudge between the Agagites and the Jews. He decides instead to wipe out the entire Jews in the region.

Racism and hatred are the real plots in the Esther story - one man using his political office to seek revenge and annihilation on an entire nation. He plots a genocide, and he got the king to sign his wish into law. Don't forget that this nation is, indeed, governed by the egos of a few men.

Mordecai and the rest of the Israelite people have heard of the decree, and they are mourning, but Esther is yet unaware. So he sends word to Esther for her to intervene on behalf of the Jews. Meanwhile, until now, Esther's real identity as a Jew is still unknown to the king and his officials.

There's another law in the palace that forbids anyone from seeing the king except on invitation. So Esther tries to explain this to Mordecai but he, in turn, reminds her that she is not exempted from this death sentence, even as queen.

On this note, Esther plots a grand approach for making her request and for defending the people of Israel from their enemy.

WHAT CAN WE LEARN?

1. Mentorship

Don't forget where we started. Esther is an orphan girl, a survivor who has just escaped death in a war and was raised by her cousin. That background is enough to keep Esther grounded for life, she has one thing going for her and it was her looks.

Everything about your life can become a strategic tool for your life's turnaround if only you learn how best to use that tool.

I was going to title the lesson, God Can Use Anybody and that would be true, except that it doesn't give a full picture. The full picture is that there are terms and conditions for God to use "anybody."

Esther was beautiful. She could have used this beauty in some other unprofitable ways but by submitting herself to the mentorship and guidance of a more experienced Mordecai, she won.

Also, during the preparations for the beauty pageant, we see Esther's willingness to submit to the leadership of Hegai - the king's eunuch in charge of the preparation. Each maiden was permitted to bring in with her anything she felt would help her to be more attractive. Esther went in there with only the things that Hegai advised.

You too can be used by God if you will do the right things. Your destiny requires the right interplay of people, places, and events to bring it to fulfillment.

2. Faith with works work.

Mordecai and Esther both believe in divine providence and the ability of God to send deliverance for Israel. Yet they both do not leave things to play out in blind faith. They prayed and Esther took action.

Prayer works, but people must add actions to their prayers.

Prayer goes hand-in-hand with thinking. As you pray, you must be willing and able to hear from God to reveal a strategy for whatever it is you are praying about.

3. Preparation

Imagine that your entire nation's existence is dependent on one presentation that you have to make and you only get one shot at this. How would you prepare?

Esther took a minimum of about 3 days to prepare to make her request.

4. Tact and Wit - You Need Those.

Esther displays tact and emotional intelligence in her approach to the king. Even when the king makes an offer up to half of his kingdom, she stays with her plan.

We know from the story that this king is not a very rational guy. He judges things based on his level of excitement so Esther deployed this knowledge to her advantage. She prepared a banquet and invited the king before making her request.

5. Hatred & Pride Blinds People.

When Haman walked into the palace that morning, he intended to receive permission for the execution of Mordecai, the one he hates. The king on the other hand was getting ready to throw a royal reception in honour of Mordecai, and he asked Haman for the right prescriptions.

Haman is so selfish that he never bothered to inquire about whom this honour was meant for. He simply thought it for himself.

Haman was hanged on the very pole he set up for Mordecai. Do not be deceived, you will reap what you sow as God cannot be mocked.

Finally, let us end our lesson by taking note of the fact that the Esther story is one filled with political intrigues. What other political lessons can we learn from this story?

REVIEW QUESTIONS:

1. Imagine that your entire nation's existence is dependent on one presentation that you have to make and you only get one shot at this. How would you prepare?

_____

_____

_____

_____

2. In what area of your life will you seek mentorship?

_____

_____

_____

_____

3. Would you consider yourself politically aware?

_____

_____

_____

_____

4. How will you apply the lessons from Esther's story?

_____

_____

_____

_____

NOTE TO PARENTS:

Esther is introduced in this story as an orphan, so not much is known about her parents. However, we see her cousin, Mordecai, stepping into the role of both parent and mentor to Esther. There is a lot to learn from this including for those who have kids that are not biologically theirs.

That child in your foster care is as much a person as your biological children, and they too have a purpose, a calling, and a destiny to fulfill.

NOTES

7. DANIEL - AND THE THREE HEBREW BOYS

Reference: The Book of Daniel

Daniel is one of the bible heroes with a book named after him. His name means, 'God is my Judge' and he was only a teenager when Nebuchadnezzar, the king of Babylon invaded his native home of Jerusalem and carried him away along with other slaves.

Among the slaves taken into captivity in the story, four young men are highlighted. They are Daniel and his three friends - Hananiah, Mishael, and Azariah. It was King Nebuchadnezzar who changed their names to Shedrack, Meshach and Abednego. Daniel's name was also changed to Belteshazzar. Note that these four guys are not the only ones taken into slavery in Babylon, but their lives and choices are the most remarkable. That's a quick lesson in setting yourself apart and making an impact in your generation.

So in the story of Daniel, we will also see the life of his friends. The most popular stories about them are the one about the furnace and the story of the lion's den. By the time that Daniel was thrown into the den, he was already more than 80 years old, but in the words of Kris Langham, "It is not the moment of victory that makes a man. It is the years of challenges and trials, faithfulness, friendship, humility, and integrity of a life lived out for God."

What is it about these four, young and inexperienced boys that brought them to prominence in a foreign land?

WHAT CAN WE LEARN?

Let's begin at chapter 1 of the book of Daniel:

1. The Qualification for Leadership

Then the king ordered Ashpenaz, chief of his court officials, to bring into the king's service some of the Israelites from the royal family and the nobility— young men without any physical defect, handsome, showing aptitude for every kind of learning, well informed, quick to understand, and qualified to serve in the king's palace. He was to teach them the language and literature of the Babylonians (Daniel 1:3-4).

What would it take to make the list as a member of the president's cabinet?

Noble Character

While you may not be born from a royal family, the ethics of nobility can be learned and imbibed. In Proverbs 31, we read the advice that a mother gave to his son, many years before he became king. Verse 4 reads, "It is not for kings, O Lemuel. It is not for kings..."

Nobility can be learnt. There is a lifestyle of royalty and if you would take time to cultivate that lifestyle, you will attract the office and recognition that come with it.

"Without any blemish, well-favored in appearance." (AMPC)

Your appearance matters. You cannot be on your way to royalty if you keep looking like peasants and urchins on the street. In every profession, there are standards for appearance. Doctors, nurses, engineers, lawyers, pilots, diplomats, sea divers, astronauts, waiters, etc.

If you decide what your goal is in life, you need to dress the part. Take care of your looks. This includes your personal hygiene, grooming, dressing, and accessories. The popular saying holds true, dress the way you want to be addressed.

"Showing an aptitude for every kind of learning, well informed, quick to understand..."

Intelligence and learning is a skill that you can learn. In an age of abundant information, you cannot afford to be ignorant. You must develop the skill for knowledge gathering. Make a habit not to answer important matters with "I don't know." You should know and if you truly do not know, find out about that matter.

In Daniel 2, the king needed an urgent interpretation for his dream and no one could tell it. When Daniel was asked, he asked the king to give him some time so he could tell the dream.

Leaders are readers. They are well informed. They develop a taste for knowledge. It is important to strive for mastery in a particular field, but also have a penchant for knowing something about all other fields.

"...qualified to serve."

Leadership is about service. To become a true leader, you must be willing to commit to serving others. A servant leader is able to inspire and lead people towards achieving a vision. Service gives you influence over the ones you serve.

Strong leaders serve while others want only to be served. You should constantly look for ways in which you can be of help to people, in school or at work. Zig Ziglar once said, "You will get all you want in life if you help enough other people get what they want."

Jesus said, "He who is greatest among you shall be your servant."

2. Competence (Wisdom and Intelligence).

"And in all matters of wisdom and understanding about which the king examined them, he found them ten times better than all the magicians and astrologers who were in all his realm."

"There is a man in your kingdom who is the Spirit of the Holy God. And in the days of your father, light and understanding and wisdom, like the wisdom of the gods, were found in him; and King Nebuchadnezzar your father—your father the king—made him chief of the magicians, astrologers, Chaldeans, and soothsayers."

If you are going to succeed in any environment, you have to have these qualities. More so if that environment is a foreign culture and even more in a palace. This was the first requirement that Nebuchadnezzar gave for their selection.

In Daniel 1:17, we are told that God gave them these gifts, but Daniel and friends did not leave these gifts at the level of mere gifts. They went on to develop themselves.

A skill is a learned ability and comes from training and practice. Don't just have gifts. Process your gifts and talents into skills. Only then can you put a price on your abilities. Only then will you be able to earn the respect of locals and foreigners alike.

It was this attribute that kept Daniel in a leadership position for four different kings (Nebuchadnezzar, Belshazzar, Darius, and Cyrus), in what was over 70 years of the captivity in Babylon.

3. Excellence

With wisdom and intelligence comes excellence. Excellence refers to the desire and quality of doing the best with the gifts and abilities that we have. It is a commitment to making things better than we found them. Stop rushing through things and leaving them half-done. Determine to finish your projects and finish them well.

"Then this Daniel distinguished himself above the governors and satraps because an excellent spirit was in him; and the king gave thought to set him over the whole realm." (Daniel 6:3)

Excellence distinguishes you. Even in the midst of opposition, everyone is attracted to excellence.

But excellence requires time and energy in applying our gifts and skills to the task at hand. Excellent people pay attention to the details of their work. Quality can be boring when it is in the works, but when it is done, its value is priceless.

4. Character and Conviction

The Babylonians were determined to change the values and way of thinking of Daniel and his friends. They began by changing their names. The names were carefully chosen to remind them about the worship of a God different from the God of Israel. Shedrack was named after the sun god - Aku, Meshach was named after the moon god, and Abednego meant servant of Nego. Daniel was renamed Belteshazzar after the god Bel.

Then they were given a new kind of education in the Babylonian occultic customs.

The Jews had food laws, there were guidelines on what not to eat, what to eat and how those foods were to be prepared. Now the Jewish boys are in a new place and they have to make a choice about eating a new kind of diet.

It is at this point that Daniel spoke up. "Daniel purposed in his heart that he would not defile himself with the portion of the king's delicacies, nor with the wine which he drank; therefore he requested of the chief of the eunuchs that he might not defile himself."

For others, this could be "just food", but for Daniel and his friends, this was about their hearts and a conviction to stand by their principles, even as teenagers, far away from home and parental influence.

Also, note the humility with which Daniel makes his case. He doesn't argue with the official over him, rather, he proposes a deal. How often do we offend other people and even insult those in authority simply because we do not agree with their position or opinion? Daniel is smart, emotionally intelligent, and understands that every disagreement must not lead to a quarrel.

5. Integrity

Daniel's integrity is impeccable. Daniel is one of the very few bible characters that is faultless, at least, according to the records. He is not just gifted with wisdom and interpretation of dreams, Daniel is committed to a life of righteousness.

According to the bible timeline, Daniel lived for over 80 years and was in leadership positions for most of those years, yet there is no dent in his integrity.

Daniel was so clean that when some of the other leaders wanted to trap him, the only option they had was to make it illegal to pray.

6. Devotion

Speaking of prayer, Daniel was definitely a man of prayer. It is recorded that he prayed with a schedule and in a place. Daniel was devoted to God.

It was Daniel who 'invented' the 21 days of fasting and prayer. A practice that has gone on over centuries to impact the entire Christendom and even other religions of the world.

This is despite the fact that there were no Jewish temples in Babylon. No one was calling for prayer meetings and worship services. Daniel was a slave.

That decision to "not defile himself with the portion of the king's delicacies, nor with the wine which he drank;" is what has given rise to something known today as "The Daniel Fast" in many faiths. We see it again in Daniel 10 where he fasted for three weeks (21 days).

The Daniel Fast is a kind of fast that focuses on eating vegetables and fruits leaving out things like meat, other sources of protein, and drinks. It is a type of fast that removes "pleasant foods" in pursuit of prayer and devotion to God.

7. Relationships

It is not likely that Daniel would have achieved all he did without the help of his three friends. This is not a major highlight of the Daniel story but do not miss it.

When the kind had his troubling dream and no one could tell it. Daniel asked for time and went back to his friends.

There is power in having a band of friends, an inner circle who share your values and can stand by you when life gets difficult. When you win, they are also there to celebrate with you without any jealousy or bitterness.

REVIEW QUESTIONS:

1. What kind of choices can you make today, to set yourself apart from your peers?

_____

_____

_____

2. Describe some of the dangers of pride as seen in the book of Daniel.

_____

_____

_____

3. Have you ever lived in an environment different from your upbringing, culture, and values? Were you able to maintain your identity or did you mix with the crowd?

_____

_____

_____

4. Can you think of a reason why many people shy away from excellence?

_____

_____

_____

_____

NOTE TO PARENTS:

Daniel's parents are not mentioned in the bible story. However, we can observe from the first chapter, the requirements stated for the selection of Daniel and his friends;

"Young men in whom there was no blemish, but good-looking, gifted in all wisdom, possessing knowledge and quick to understand, who had ability to serve in the king's palace, and whom they might teach the language and literature of the Chaldeans."

The young men were taken from Israel when they were still boys, and several other children would have been taken into captivity too who did not meet these requirements. The traits listed were aptitudes that they would have picked up from home.

Parents can choose to prepare their children for a life of independence, away from home, bearing in mind that you will not always be there with/for them.

Proverbs 22:6 suggests "Train up a child in the way he should go, And when he is old he will not depart from it."

NOTES

8. MARY — THE MOTHER OF JESUS

Reference: Luke 1 - 2.

The name Mary was a common name in Israel at the time of this story so to be clear, we are looking at one Mary - the mother of Jesus.

For the records, there are seven persons known as Mary in the Bible: Mary Magdalene, Mary of Bethany, Mary the mother of James, Mary the mother of John Mark, Mary of Cleophas, Mary of Rome, and Mary the mother of Jesus.

The Story of Mary the mother of Jesus (we'll just call her Mary) is one that you may have been familiar with because it has always been told as the Christmas story.

Mary was a teenage girl (most historians believe she was between 16 & 18) engaged to a man named Joseph. One day, she is visited by the angel Gabriel, and Gabriel said she has been chosen to give birth to Jesus. At that time, there have been lots of prophecies about the birth of Jesus - the Messiah. Every Jew in the city knew this prophecy and they were looking forward to its fulfillment when Mary got the news that the Messiah was going to be born by her. This was an enormous responsibility.

She reminded the angel (in case he was not aware) that she was still a virgin, no husband, no experience in parenting, etc. "How shall these things be?" Mary asked.

The story of a pregnant virgin would bring shame in the city and this almost cost her her relationship with Joseph. Mary's response was "...Let it be to me according to your word."

The baby in Mary's womb is a picture of God's vision for your life. It is a picture of a solution, an invention, a business, etc. that the world is waiting for and it is coming through you.

What does it take to be used by God in your generation? What are the requirements for carrying a responsibility like raising and nurturing God's own son?

WHAT CAN WE LEARN?

1. God's Presence

Notice the greeting from Angel Gabriel: "Greetings, you who are highly favored! The Lord is with you."

There is a connection between 'highly favoured,' and 'the Lord is with you.' God's presence and His favour go hand-in-hand. If you want the favour, pursue His presence.

We learn more of this in the book of Hebrews."...he who comes to God must believe that He is and that He is a rewarder of those who diligently seek Him."

First, you must come to the presence of God (where HE IS with you) and then you can be sure of being highly favoured (His rewards), but if all you seek is the reward, the gifts, and favours, you are most likely going to miss out on everything.

Mary had a life of devotion and relationship with God which is of course why she entertained the presence of an angel. It looks as if she was troubled by the message of the angel, but not by his presence, something she was probably acquainted with. And she expresses her devotion through the songs she sang later at Elizabeth's house. That song is popularly referred to as the Magnificat.

2. Prayer

How do you 'cultivate' the presence of God or like a book I read many years ago, 'Practice the Presence of God'?

It is through prayer. What is prayer?

Prayer is communication with God. Like every other form of communication, it is a two-way street meaning that you must also be able to hear from the other person as much as you speak. Learn to speak to God in your own words and let him talk back to you. It is that simple.

You can talk to God at any time of the day, and you can create a special time of meeting with him. Just like you can talk to your parents or friends at any time, but you also have special hangouts and mealtimes when you can chat for longer periods. Do the same with God. He wants to hang out with you, this is called 'devotion.' In your time and place of devotion, do three things; read your bible, worship Him with words or songs, and pray. You do the talking in prayer and worship and He talks back to you through His words in the bible and sometimes, in your heart and thoughts.

The human spirit is designed to function under the atmosphere of God's presence, so make prayer a habit.

Mary was committed to a life prayer. We read many times in Luke 1-2 that she 'pondered in her heart' and in Acts 1:14 where she was with other disciples praying.

3. Virtue & Character

Mary was not just a beautiful young lady, she had virtue and she was bold in communicating her moral position even to an angel. Mary could have simply accepted all that the angel said because, come to think of it, this was an angel. But no, she wasn't going to accept a blanket prophecy that was clearly going to violate her moral stance.

It may seem today that virtue and morality are old-fashioned and out of vogue, but that is a deception. It is still a big deal among those who desire to do great things for God and for their generation. Be clear on your personal values and be ready to stand boldly by those values before anybody.

The other part of this speaks to the strength of Mary's character. We see this in the question that Mary asked, "How shall this be...?"

Another young woman today would gladly scream "Amen!" at a prophecy declared in church, on a Sunday morning, or a crusade ground. There may be nothing wrong in shouting 'amen' but stop and consider how these things will be.

Asking the question, "How?" will reveal a number of things, including what specific actions you may need to take or whether there would be compromises required of you to make.

Dear young person, ask questions. The quality of questions you ask will determine the quality of life you live.

4. Friendships

The story of Mary and Elizabeth is a representation of true friendship. Elizabeth was a friend and prayer partner of Mary. They had shared values, and this made it easy for both ladies to share their dreams and visions with each other.

Mary's vision was bigger than Elizabeth's, more so, Elizabeth's child, even though he was 6 months older, was going to be a servant to Mary's child. In a dishonest relationship, this would have been a cause for envy, but Elizabeth was genuinely happy for Mary and both were excited about what they have been called to do.

In choosing your friends, it is important that you all have shared values. Be genuinely happy for one another no matter who has the big idea. Your friend should be those that you can run to when you feel confused about the turn of events.

5. Patience

The fact that Mary was going to be pregnant for nine months required patience. How was she feeling knowing all that has been said about this baby in her womb?

You have a destiny to fulfill, but that destiny will require a process to come through. There are young people today who do not wish to go through the process. We all want it to happen fast or 'sharp-sharp' like we say. The era of instant messaging and social media has not helped us too. When you see the flashy images on the gram and desire to have the same experience and lifestyle, consider for a moment what the process is for the things you desire.

The time of pregnancy is not idle time either. Waiting time is preparation time. In your patience, do the things that you need to do. Get an education. Finish school. Seek mentorship. Get an internship. Travel. Volunteer somewhere. And don't forget, be happy. Mary was joyful all this while. There is so much you can do in your waiting time. Keep getting ready for your big day.

6. Sacrifice

The story of a pregnant virgin would bring shame in the city and this almost cost her her relationship with Joseph. God intervened, but Mary already accepted this as the price for fulfilling her calling.

When you decide to do something great with your life, be prepared for the sacrifice that comes along. It will cost you some friends, and some of what you consider as a good life. You can no longer live like every other 'normal' young person in your school or neighbourhood. It will cost you time and most of that time, you will be alone.

REVIEW QUESTIONS:

1. Have you ever waited for something that you were promised? What was your attitude while you waited?

_____

_____

_____

_____

2. What destiny are you expecting to fulfill for God?

_____

_____

_____

_____

3. Which of your friends would you go to share with, when you have an idea or inspiration from God?

_____

_____

_____

_____

4. How will you apply the lessons from Mary's story?

_____

_____

_____

_____

NOTE TO PARENTS:

The story of Mary and Elizabeth paints a picture of friendship. However, we know from the story that Elizabeth was much more elderly than Mary, and we are not told about Mary's parents. The role that Mary played as an emotional support and prayer partner is something that most parents can take away from the story. Let your children come to you with their major life experiences and encounters.

In the face of an embarrassing experience, Elizabeth provided protection for Mary. Mary lived in her house for the first three months of her pregnancy. Even though both were going to be first-time moms, Elizabeth had more experience in family life and womanhood.

No matter how great children and their ideas can be, they need to be nurtured properly until the time when those ideas will be birthed. Young people need parents who can properly discern their gifts and callings and provide mentorship for reaching those goals.

NOTES

9. JESUS — THE SON OF GOD

Reference Luke 2:39-52

Born in one of the most obscure circumstances, a little boy from the little town of Bethlehem claiming to be God's own son and the saviour of mankind, rose to become the most important person in all of human history. At the time of his death, He was only 33 years old.

The bible is silent about His teenage years, but have you ever wondered what Jesus was like as a teenager? It is also believed that some of Jesus disciples were teenagers.

Read the passage above and let's find out.

From that short passage, we learn a lot about the personality and character of Jesus as a boy. The secret of Jesus' success as a young man is summarized in two verses;

"And the Child grew and became STRONG IN SPIRIT, filled with WISDOM; and the GRACE of God was upon Him."

"And Jesus INCREASED IN WISDOM and STATURE, and in FAVOUR with God and men."

1. Devotion

Jesus learnt about a life of devotion and spirituality from his parents - Mary and Joseph. Beginning at verse 21, Mary and Joseph did all that was required of the law for the baby Jesus. It appears that they continued to live this kind of life, because in Luke 4:16, we are told that Jesus had become accustomed to visiting the synagogue.

When Jesus was 12 years old, his family was in Jerusalem for the Passover, Jesus' parents left the festival unknowingly without him. They found him after three days and he asked them a question, "Did you not know that I must be about My Father's business?"

If you have misplaced Jesus in your life, for any reason, and you need to find Him, go back to His Father's house and you will find Him there. Jesus is always hanging out there.

It is by this commitment to a life of devotion that Jesus became strong in spirit.

2. Wisdom

Jesus was not only filled with wisdom, He increased in wisdom and that implies that he continued to learn. When his parents lost him at the temple, they found him "sitting in the midst of the doctors, both hearing them, and asking them questions."

Jesus would have continued to pursue an education and to improve himself because, later on we read about Jesus many years later that He taught in the synagogue, and the men were marveled that they asked said, "Where did this Man get this wisdom."

Jesus also became a carpenter (or a furniture maker) like his father, so not only did he gain intellectual and spiritual wisdom, He also learnt a skill.

3. Humility

It takes humility to learn. It takes humility to ask questions. It takes humility to be teachable. Truly wise people are humble people.

Jesus submitted himself, humility to learning from the doctors and teachers of the law in his youth.

He also submitted himself to learning the skill and craft of his father, Joseph.

This same humility is shown in the famous feet washing of his disciples. He showed through His life that the path to honour is through service and humility.

"Pride goes before destruction, And a haughty spirit before a fall." - Proverbs 16:18

4. Hard work.

A carpenter's job is not that of a lazy man. Jesus worked with his hands and helped his family as a young boy. He was also developing his mind. He was hanging out with doctors and professors of His time meaning that He was not intellectually lazy. He loved to read.

5. Stature

Back in the scripture we read that Jesus increased in stature. Stature here would refer to his physical development.

Jesus paid attention to his health. To increase in stature could have meant a physical development of his muscles. He paid attention to things like exercise and being fit.

6. Favour with God.

The favour of God is also known as the grace of God. It is the total expression of God's kindness towards a person. It is God helping us in our ventures and endeavours.

The grace of God is also what we can rely on when we go through difficulties in life. In the popular song "You Raise Me Up", Josh Groban wrote:

When I am down and, oh my soul, so weary
When troubles come and my heart burdened be
Then, I am still and wait here in the silence
Until you come and sit awhile with me

You raise me up, so I can stand on mountains
You raise me up, to walk on stormy seas
I am strong, when I am on your shoulders
You raise me up... To more than I can be

Grace is unmerited favour implying that we cannot do anything to deserve it. However, grace can be courted and cultivated. It is evident that Jesus cultivated this grace by his life of devotion to God.

7. Favour with man.

Jesus had favour with God and with man. That shows a balance between His spiritual life (with God) and His social life (with man).

One would think that because Jesus had a divine call, he wouldn't need the favour of men. In reality Jesus' call and assignment on earth required his collaboration with men for it to be fulfilled.

All through this book, we have seen the place of relationships in the fulfillment of different destinies. To find favour with men is about cultivating the right kind of relationships and networks.

People are the richest resource you will ever have. To succeed in life therefore, you must learn to be a people person.

"A man *who has* friends must himself be friendly..." Proverbs 18:24

Here are a few things you can do to improve your social life:

- Be kind to people.
- Develop your self-confidence.
- Encourage people.
- Be genuinely interested in the good of others.
- Show love and give. As much as possible give your time, give you talent and give your treasure (money) where necessary.
- Serve people.

Be a people person.

REVIEW QUESTIONS:

1. What aspects of your life do you need to develop more? (Spirit, Wisdom, Stature, Favour).

_____

_____

_____

_____

2. Which of your relationships do you need to strengthen? (Family and Friends)

_____

_____

_____

_____

3. What will you do to become a more friendly person?

_____

_____

_____

_____

4. How will you apply the lessons from Jesus' Story?

_____

_____

_____

_____

NOTE TO PARENTS:

From our reference scripture, we find Jesus and His parents had some misunderstanding. "As they returned," from the Passover Feast in Jerusalem, "Jesus lingered behind in Jerusalem."

Jesus had been missing from His parents for three days before they found Him in the temple. The conversation that happened when they found him is even more interesting. Mary, like every mother would, expressed her concerns about the situation, but Jesus responded like the typical teenager response, "Why are you looking for me?"

The boy doesn't quite understand his parents' agitations. As far as he was concerned, nothing happened.

While they were kids, they did everything you said, no questions asked, but as teenagers young people begin to seek their own unique interest and identity. They start forming new relationships outside of home and those relationships begin to matter more to them than the relationship they have with their parents.

This is usually not a premeditated slight on the authority of the parent, but a normal process growing up and finding themselves.

The next question Jesus asked holds a key that parents should pay attention to. He said, "Did you not know that I must be about My Father's business?"

According to the boy, Mary should have known where to find him instead of declaring him missing.

Parents can play the role of a mentor in helping a teenager discover their unique identity, personality, and interests. You must be willing to step aside from being their closest parley while guiding them to find new relationships.

This is where exposure and environments matter. We typically find and choose our friends from the environments we have been exposed to. Mary and Joseph had done a good job putting Jesus in the environment that nurtured his destiny. They built a custom of going to the temple. It was only natural that that would be his choice spot for hanging out.

"Train up a child in the way he should go, And when he is old he will not depart from it."

Begin with purpose discovery. After discovery comes development. Young people will always choose friends based on who they think they are and what they want to become.

Dear parents, do you know where to find your teenager?

NOTES

NOTES

FINAL WORDS

In writing this book, I wanted to highlight the life principles that distinguished each of these bible characters.

As young people, we desire success, and rightly so. Everyone who desires success must make him/herself a student of same. And if you are going to be a student of success, you must study the lives and profiles of successful people.

The bible is between 3,500 and 1,900 years old making it about the oldest books in history. The stories in the bible span a period of about 1,500 years. Yet many of the stories and principles found therein hold true to this day.

If you were looking for time-tested wisdom and principles of success, who would you prefer to mentor you? A 30-year-old or a 3,000-year-old?

With nearly half of the world's population under the age of 25, our world today is in need of youngsters who stand for something. Joseph rose above hate and sexual temptation, David showed exemplary courage, wit, and skill in face of danger. Daniel was an example of integrity and excellence. Timothy found the ultimate adventure in leadership.

You as a student of success must learn to combine these lessons and forge your own strategy in a world that is hell-bent on redefining the essence of youth.

"Through desire a man having separated himself, seeketh [and] *intermeddleth* with all wisdom;"

Desire and pursue after sound wisdom and knowledge. Utilize every proper means to attain it; you must be willing to separate yourself from the vain entanglements of youth and give yourself to constant improvement through reading, study, meditation, and prayer.

Cheers to your success!

About the Author

Chiedozie Eze is a personal development coach for teenagers and young people. He is an entrepreneur with experience in human resource, logistics, and supply-chain management.

Chiedozie is a public speaker, trainer, and writer. He is the author of *Game Plan - A Life Plan Workbook for Young People, My Book of Affirmations,* and three other e-books on personal development.

He is a graduate of Electrical/Electronics Engineering and a certified safety professional. He has also received advanced leadership certifications from several institutions and a leadership award from the Akwa-Ibom State Government for his contributions to the MDGs Advocacy Project in the state.

For over 10 years, Chiedozie has had experience in the nonprofit sector with a focus on youth development, communications, and strategic leadership.

He is the Founder of Teen Success Academy, a coaching outfit equipping young people with tools for personal discovery, confidence, and success.

Chiedozie conducts seminars and training for young people, parents, and teachers. He is the host of the **360 SUCCESS BOOTCAMP,** a one-month virtual Bootcamp coming up in August with the theme: **THRIVE** (Training Highly Resourceful Individuals with Value & Excellence).